LET'S LEARN ABOUT
COMPUTER SCIENCE

HARDWARE

Jeff Mapua

Enslow Publishing
101 W. 23rd Street
Suite 240
New York, NY 10011
USA

enslow.com

WORDS TO KNOW

computer An electric-powered machine that can save, find, and work with data.

data Information that is used in a computer.

device An object that does a job.

graphics Pictures that are made by a computer on a screen.

hardware The parts of a computer that you can touch.

keyboard A set of keys with letters, numbers, and symbols. It is used for typing.

microprocessor The part of the computer that handles information and completes tasks.

monitor A computer screen.

motherboard The part of the computer that connects the different parts of hardware.

mouse A small device that is moved by hand. It is used to select or move things on the screen.

task A job.

CONTENTS

People of all ages can use a computer.

Computers

Have you ever used a **computer**? These machines can do many things. People use them to send email, shop online, or play games.

FAST FACT

Smartphones and tablets are kinds of computers.

**There are many parts
inside a computer
that help it work.**

Computer Parts

A computer is made up of many parts. These parts all do different things. Together, they make a computer work. These parts include a screen and a **motherboard**.

Fast Fact

The first electronic computers were as big as a room!

This man is working on a computer.
He is fixing the hardware.

Hardware

Computers have parts you can touch and parts you cannot touch. You can touch a keyboard. You cannot touch a computer game. The parts you can touch are called **hardware**.

FAST FACT

The earliest computers used lots of electricity.

Computer keyboards do not just have letters and numbers. They also have symbols and commands.

Keyboard

People type on a **keyboard**. They can enter numbers and letters into a computer. The keys tell the computer what to do.

FAST FACT

Not all keyboards are the same. Different countries have different letters on their keyboards.

A mouse makes it easy to move around a computer screen.

Mouse

A computer **mouse** lets you select and move items on the screen. You move or click a mouse with your hand. Then the computer moves the same way on the screen.

FAST FACT

The first computer mouse was made of wood.

A computer monitor can show words, pictures, or videos.

Screens and Monitors

A computer screen is part of the hardware. It shows words and **graphics** made by a computer. A computer screen is also called a **monitor**.

A computer hard drive. This is a very important part of a computer.

Hard Drive

The hard drive is the main piece of hardware. It saves **data** on the computer. Files and programs, like computer games, are saved on the hard drive.

Fast Fact

Data on a hard drive is saved even when the computer is turned off.

A worker makes microprocessors at a factory.

Microprocessor

The **microprocessor** is the "brain" of a computer. It is a small chip inside the computer. It handles the information that goes into and out of a computer.

FAST FACT

Computers, phones, and televisions all use a microprocessor.

The motherboard
connects all of the
computer parts.

Motherboard

The **motherboard** connects all of the hardware inside a computer. The microprocessor, hard drive, and other parts connect to the motherboard. It is the "backbone" of the computer.

Fast Fact

The first motherboard came out in 1981.

Activity
Fun with Hardware

MATERIALS
notebook
pencil
old computer
tools

Here are some ways to learn more about hardware:

- Take a look for yourself! Find an old computer

or electronic device to open up. Use tools to look inside a computer. Make sure you get an adult to help!

- Tell the difference between hardware and software. List the parts of a computer that you can touch and the parts you cannot touch.

- Check out the Learn More section of this book for a website that lets you practice naming the parts of a computer.

LEARN MORE

Books

Liukas, Linda. *Hello Ruby: Journey Inside the Computer.* New York, NY: Feiwel & Friends, 2017.

Small, Cathleen. *What Are Hardware and Software?* New York, NY: Britannica, 2017.

Zuchora-Walske, Christine. *What's Inside My Computer?* Minneapolis, MN: Lerner, 2016.

Websites

Kids Online Click-N-Learn
www.kids-online.net / learn / click / table. html
Point and click on the different parts of the computer to learn more about them.

Raspberry Pi
www.raspberrypi.org
Check out these fun computer hardware projects to do with an adult! Projects include creating your own musical equipment and gaming system.

INDEX

Published in 2019 by Enslow Publishing, LLC.
101 W. 23rd Street, Suite 240, New York, NY 10011

Copyright © 2019 by Enslow Publishing, LLC.

Library of Congress Cataloging-in-Publication Data

Names: Mapua, Jeff, author.
Title: Hardware / Jeff Mapua.
Description: New York : Enslow Publishing, [2019] | Series: Let's learn about computer science | Includes bibliographical references and index. |
Audience: Grades K to 4.
Identifiers: LCCN 2018004905| ISBN 9781978501829 (library bound) | ISBN 9781978502277 (pbk.) | ISBN 9781978502284 (6 pack)
Subjects: LCSH: Computer input-output equipment—Juvenile literature. |Computer engineering—Juvenile literature.
Classification: LCC TK7887.5 .M36 2019 | DDC 004—dc23

LC record available at https://lccn.loc.gov/2018004905

Printed in the United States of America

Photos Credits: Cover, p. 1 DenisProduction.com/ Shutterstock.com; pp. 2, 3, 4, 24 Best-Backgrounds/ Shutterstock.com; p. 4 Monkey Business Images/ Shutterstock.com; p. 6 Kitch Bain/Shutterstock.com; p. 8 vystekimages/Shutterstock.com; p. 10 James Sedgemore/ Shutterstock.com; p. 12 Catalin Petolea/Shutterstock.com; p. 14 Andrey_Popov/Shutterstock.com; p. 16 stockfoto/ Shutterstock.com; p. 18 franz12/Shutterstock.com; p. 20 Naumov S/Shutterstock.com; p. 22 JJ pixs/Shutterstock.com; interior design elements (laptop) ArthurStock/Shutterstock. com, (flat screen computer) Aleksandrs Bondars/ Shutterstock.com.